SO-AHD-262

Warwick Studies in Industrial Relations
General Editors: George Bain, Hugh Clegg,
Allan Flanders

RACE AND INDUSTRIAL CONFLICT

Warwick Studies in Industrial Relations

MALCOLM RIMMER

Race and Industrial Conflict

A Study in a Group of Midland Foundries

HEINEMANN EDUCATIONAL BOOKS

LONDON

Heinemann Educational Books Ltd
LONDON EDINBURGH MELBOURNE TORONTO
SINGAPORE JOHANNESBURG AUCKLAND IBADAN
HONG KONG NAIROBI NEW DELHI KUALA LUMPUR

ISBN 0 435 85765 7

Published by Heinemann Educational Books Ltd
48 Charles Street, London, W1X 8AH

Printed in Great Britain by
Willmer Brothers Limited, Birkenhead

Editors' Foreword

Warwick University's first undergraduates were admitted in 1965. The teaching of industrial relations began a year later, and in 1967 a one-year graduate course leading to an M.A. in Industrial Relations was introduced. At about the same time a grant from the Clarkson Trustees allowed a beginning to be made on a research project concerned with several aspects of industrial relations in selected Coventry plants.

In 1970 the Social Science Research Council established three Research Units, one of them being the Industrial Relations Research Unit at Warwick. The Unit took over the Coventry project and developed others, including studies of union growth, union organisation, occupational labour markets, coloured immigrants in industry, ideologies of 'fairness' in industrial relations and the effects of the Industrial Relations Act.

This monograph series is intended to form the main vehicle for the publication of the results of the Unit's projects, of the research carried out by staff teaching industrial relations in the University, and, where it merits publication, of the work of graduate students. Some of these results will, of course, be published as articles, and some in the end may constitute full-scale volumes. But the monograph is the most apt form for much of our work. Industrial relations research is concerned with assembling and analysing evidence much of which cannot be succinctly summarised in tables and graphs, so that an adequate presentation of findings can easily take too much space for an article. On the other hand, even with a major project which will in the end lead to one or more books, there is often an advantage in publishing interim results as monographs. This is particularly true where the project deals, as do several of the industrial relations studies at Warwick, with problems of current interest for which employers, trade unionists and governments are anxiously seeking solutions.

Mr Rimmer's study of Race and Industrial Conflict deals with such a topic. The increasing number of coloured immigrant employees in Britain has brought a growing number of instances of industrial conflict which are apparently complicated by racial elements. Mr Rimmer examines the consequences of the development of ethnic work groups in a situation where—as is common in Britain—many of the rules of industrial relations are established by custom and practice. He shows how these consequences may lead to conflict, and examines the relevance of ideas of prejudice and absorption to situations of this kind. His findings hold interest for managers and trade unionists as well as for students of industrial relations, of industrial sociology and of race relations.

GEORGE BAIN
HUGH CLEGG
ALLAN FLANDERS

Contents

List of Abbreviations

AEF

Amalgamated Union of Engineering and Foundry Workers. In 1968 the AUFW (Amalgamated Union of Foundry Workers) amalgamated with the AEU (Amalgamated Engineering Union) to become the foundry section of the AEF. Since 1970 further amalgamations with DATA (Draughtsmen's and Allied Technicians' Association) and the CEU (Constructional Engineering Union) have brought into existence the AUEW (Amalgamated Union of Engineering Workers), but at the time of this study the union was the AEF, so this title is used.

ASTMS

Association of Scientific, Technical and Managerial Staffs.

CIR

Commission on Industrial Relations

DE

Department of Employment

TGWU

Transport and General Workers' Union

I

Introduction

THE PURPOSE OF THE STUDY

This study sets out to examine some of the effects that ethnic work-units can have upon industrial relations. It suggests that a major effect of the employment of cohesive groups of immigrants is to undermine the informal custom-and-practice rules which have dominated many aspects of job regulation in British industry. Various consequences, including an increase in overt industrial conflict, may follow from the breakdown of such informal understandings and rules.

The study is consequently concerned with two themes: on the one hand with the detailed mechanics of the growth of normative disorder in industrial relations; and on the other hand with the nature of conflict relationships in industry between coloured immigrants, white workers and management. These two themes are expanded in the following sections in this chapter.

The bulk of the study is composed of the analysis of empirical information derived from case studies in a small foundry group. This empirical information can be presented as a four-stage process. Firstly, a large group of coloured immigrants gained employment in certain occupations in the foundries. Secondly, these immigrants developed a strong domestic trade-union organization which was closely connected with the group solidarity of the ethnic work-units. Following this the unionized immigrants became involved in conflict with both management and the white workers over the operation of informal rules. The final stage in the process was the development of formal written procedures for the avoidance of disputes. The final stage is, however, treated as a postscript. What is crucial in the process outlined above is not the final outcome in terms of a reformed system of rules governing certain aspects of job regulation, but the underlying causes of conflict.

THE NATURE OF CUSTOM AND PRACTICE

Since one of the major themes of the study is the disorder which occurs when regulation by custom and practice breaks down, it is necessary to say something about the way in which custom and practice operates and what distinguishes it from other forms of regulation.

Different methods of job regulation are usually classified by the parties who make the rules. Thus rules which are fixed in collective bargaining between management and worker representatives can be distinguished from rules which are fixed unilaterally by either management, workers or the State. Flanders[1] distinguishes two further types of external rule-making processes: trilateral regulation (where rules are made jointly by management, workers and public representatives), and social regulation (where rules derive from custom and convention).

In so far as social regulation includes custom-and-practice rules, with which this study is concerned, they fit uneasily into such a classification. In most cases their authorship is an insignificant aspect. They are often enforced by and for the benefit of parties not involved in making the rules. Furthermore, it is often difficult to say which party is responsible for making a particular rule. This can happen for two reasons. Firstly, the rule may be so old that the author is literally forgotten. More important, many of these rules have only evolved gradually in the context of a set of interactions between management and workers. A member of management may set a precedent in making an isolated decision which is not intended to be generally applicable as a rule. If the work-group finds that this isolated decision constitutes a beneficial precedent, pressures may be put upon lower management for the decision to be applied generally. At some stage, often without either party being aware of the consequences of their actions, a fully fledged rule will emerge requiring supervision and enforcement, with sanctions being applied if it is broken.

Custom-and-practice rules have often been seen as a form of unilateral regulation by workers. The most commonly studied examples have been work-group restrictions of output and determinants of manning levels in craft employment[2]. Both of these are areas where the work group or union appears to make the rules. However, in most cases even this sort of practice requires managerial approval, whether tacit or explicit, to work at all. Lower management may support apparently deviant work-group practices and norms of behaviour, either from a desire to avoid disruption, or because supervisors have become socialized into accepting the particular norms of the workers[3]. In most instances there is a sense in which custom-and-practice rules could be called 'joint'. Their existence will depend upon their acceptability to both management and workers.

A few points must be made about the way that custom-and-practice rules acquire legitimacy[4]. In internal job regulation, management does not have to appeal to custom and practice to establish a rule since its commands are legitimated under the general heading of managerial prerogative. But workers generally possess no recognized right to make rules governing their conditions of work. They must either engage in collective bargaining to establish joint rules, or find indirect methods of establishing rules. One such method it to describe practices that develop through exploitation of managerial weaknesses and aberrations as customary rules or 'custom and practice'. Particular concessions are sometimes applied out of context and individual precedents are interpreted as demonstrating the existence of a rule. Thus work-groups will use the term 'custom and practice' to establish the legitimacy of a rule that benefits them.

While much custom and practice is of this sort, it is important to realize that a great deal of custom and practice is genuinely customary. In traditional industries in particular, many of these rules are traditional and consist simply of long-standing and accepted practices. 'Custom and practice' can be both a heading under which workers and shop-stewards justify their own involvement in creating fresh rules, and a heading to cover traditional practices, which the work-group may have an interest in preserving.

In practice, where internal job regulation is unsystematic, the rules generally rest upon both types of custom and practice as well as managerial prerogative. For such an arrangement to be stable one of two conditions must be fulfilled. Either one party must dominate the other, or there must be extensive shared understandings upon the legitimacy of the rules. The importance of these shared understandings in determining the stability of custom and practice must be emphasized. Recently, a great deal of British industry has been characterized by a breakdown of these shared understandings[5] as a result of various social and economic pressures. Flanders and Fox[6] have claimed that in many cases the system of job regulation has collapsed in Britain because of conflict between group aspirations and prevailing norms. This study shows how the prevailing norms linked to the operation of custom-and-practice rules broke down because they were incompatible with the aspirations and behaviour of immigrants in ethnic work-units. The shared understandings which maintained the stability of custom-and-practice regulation in the foundries were undermined by racial factors.

RACE RELATIONS IN INDUSTRY

The previous section attempts to clarify some ideas concerning custom-and-practice job regulation—one of the major themes of the study. This section examines some ideas relating to the other theme of race relations in industry. While there has been little systematic writing on custom and practice, there is a considerable body of literature on immigrants in industry.

This study is concerned with the way in which immigrants fit into a system of job regulation which is dominated by custom-and-practice rules and understandings. Most of the other studies of immigrants in industry do not concern themselves with industrial relations factors, with the consequence that very little is known about such aspects of immigrant behaviour as their involvement in trade unions, their relations with managements in domestic bargaining or their involvement in strike activity. There have been two studies of strikes where racial factors were important[7], but the largest body of research upon immigrants in industry revolves around two concepts. Studies have concentrated either upon the pathology of race relations embodied in such concepts as prejudice or discrimination, or upon indicators of absorption which see the totality of employment relationships specifically in terms of the Eisenstadt type framework[8]. The first of these conceptual approaches seeks only to explain conflict between races in terms of perceptions of racial characteristics. At its crudest this approach may characterize all conflict between racial groups simply as the product of prejudice. Policy-oriented research upon immigrants in industry has sometimes tended to place a strong emphasis upon discovering evidence of discrimination, and proposing solutions to the problem.

The second of these conceptual approaches is concerned with establishing processes by which immigrants become absorbed by a host society. Such an approach emphasizes cultural characteristics of the immigrant and host societies and the way in which interaction between cultures can produce an integrated society. The emphasis upon structural factors in such an explanation results in a tendency to ignore attitudes towards race and the actors' perceptions of racial differences.

Both these approaches have their utility in that they can be used to explain different aspects of race relations. However, neither approach has been used satisfactorily to explain the unique problems facing immigrants that result from their involvement in industrial employment. Admittedly, most of the research has been done by social anthropologists who lacked an interest in industrial relations. This lack of interest has been reinforced by the way in which the conceptual frameworks have been employed. Writings upon trade unions and immigrants have concerned themselves almost entirely with discrimination inside unions, and the way in which the closed shop or craft restrictions can reinforce such tendencies[9]. While it is recognized that trade unions are an important institution in which integration can take place, there has been no research upon the involvement of immigrants in central trade-union activities such as bargaining, organizing and recruitment, or the maintenance of work rules.

Research employing the concept of absorption has tended to be concerned with the most obvious peculiarities of immigrants in employment. These peculiarities tend to emerge as managerial problems. Thus research has examined such issues as the training of immigrants, quotas to limit their employment, promotion to supervisory posts, and social relations with white workers[10]. Though involvement in the institutions of job regulation is an important part of the absorption process, it has generally not been studied. Perhaps industrial relations have not been seen as worthy of special study because they have been assumed to be in no way different for immigrants than for white workers. Such an assumption is not sustained by the findings of this study.

Whatever the merits of the existing race and absorption approaches, there is a case for looking at the involvement of immigrants in job regulation. Immigrants may substantially alter the operation of a system of job regulation because they have different cultural values and patterns of behaviour that may be inconsistent with the established norms underlying the system. Furthermore, the nature of their involvement in industrial relations will substantially affect their relationships with both management and white workers. It is a factor to be considered when examining either discrimination or absorption.

RESEARCH METHODS AND TECHNIQUES

Information about industrial relations, employment, and race relations was collected from several sources. The foundry management kept records of employment, earnings, overtime, labour turnover, and major disputes, but no records were kept for very long. Thus, although the information was adequate for a study at one point in time, it was not possible to trace such trends as the rate of build-up of the immigrants in the labour force. Recorded accounts

B

of disputes represented only the management's view, and this had to be balanced against accounts gained in interviews with union representatives.

In addition to this documentary evidence, the shop stewards and full-time officials of the union, all levels of management and Department of Employment (DE) officials were interviewed. The interview material was more extensive than the statistical data but was not always reliable in relation to events that had occurred some time in the past.

No questionnaires or surveys were used. Such methods could have gained useful information on a number of topics, including the origins and work experience of the immigrants, their attitudes towards management and unions, and towards work practices and rules, but the problems of communication with a labour force that could generally not speak English made them impracticable.

The Foundries : The Setting

This section looks at four topics that provide a background for the empirical material and arguments with which the study is directly concerned.

First, a description of the size, organization and general nature of the foundries is needed. In addition, technical factors, the commercial and economic environment and the organization and behaviour of management must be described, since these factors affected the conflict that occurred. Any explanation of a situation of industrial conflict is likely to be both distorted and unconvincing if a single cause is sought or offered. In this particular instance there were several factors that contributed to a period of unrest, but since the analysis is only interested in exploring one of these factors it is important to mention the others, so that they can be borne in mind for the rest of the account.

The foundries belonged to a large group controlling a number of different companies in the engineering industry. They produced grey iron castings, largely for the motor industry in the Midlands. Because of these two factors, management did not have a great deal of freedom in its handling of disputes. When strikes were in progress, there was heavy pressure from customers and the group directors to settle disputes quickly.

Four foundries belonged to the group. Two were sited close together and will be referred to as 1a and 1b, since they shared a core shop and maintenance section. The others, Nos. 2 and 3, were about half a mile away from this main block, where, in addition, the central offices were located. The total labour force, including clerical, technical and managerial staff, numbered about 950 workers, so about 200 workers were employed in each foundry. This appears to be an average figure for the Midlands, though there are still many smaller independent foundries.

The foundry buildings were very old; two of the four dated back to the First World War, and even the new ones had far from good working conditions. Foundry work is generally characterized by great extremes of temperature and a dusty atmosphere, and is frequently dangerous if workers are not sure of the correct safety precautions. In consequence, high earnings have to be paid for unskilled labour since better working conditions can easily be found. Because of this, foundry managements have been more prepared than other industries to employ immigrants, since this is the only way that severe labour shortages can be avoided.

The technical characteristics of foundry work have a considerable impact upon the social organization of the workers. To begin with, foundry work consists of several different processes which are carried out in separate shops, each largely isolated from the others. Occupational differences are emphasized where, for instance, all the dressers or core-makers are working together in groups, with little contact with the casters or moulders. Thus clear distinctions develop between occupational work-groups. The cohesion of these groups is often strengthened by the fact that they work on group bonus schemes, since their output can only be measured on a group basis. This applies both to labourers, engaged on knocking out castings, and, on some tracks, to the moulders who work in groups of eight with a group bonus. Secondly, foundry work tends to be fragmented, partly because production runs for particular castings are short, and this factor, combined with piece-work, has led to a very complicated system of piece-prices. In the absence of close managerial control, large disparities develop between foundries over prices for specific operations, even where the operation is standarized. Moreover, nearly all occupations have direct control over the pace of their work, but the interrelation of processes means that output restrictions in one section, such as the knock-out section, can disrupt work elsewhere. There are group norms concerning output, but at the time of the study these had become complicated by the breakdown of custom and practice where immigrants were employed. The immigrants tended to employ output restrictions only as a sanction. In general, they were responsive to the possibilities of increasing their earnings by increased effort. A system which depends upon the compatibility of output norms of work groups can be easily disrupted. Finally, since foundry work involves the use of hot metal, it entails much preparation and finishing. One consequence of this is that a great deal of overtime is worked. More important, however, a large number of customs develop around the handling of the metal; for instance, all the metal must be poured from a cupola before it is left for any reason. Compensatory payments have to be made, to allow for the large number of failures that can occur in the process of producing a casting, and these further complicate what is already a complex payment system. These effects of technical factors upon social and work organization are not particularly unusual, since many industries experience similar influences to those outlined above. A great deal of custom and practice is not comprehensible, however, unless the technical processes are understood, because rules are often closely related to particular technical factors.

The commercial environment of the foundries had a considerable impact upon the outcome of the various disputes that occurred. Some of these factors have been mentioned above. In addition, the profitability of the foundries declined between 1965 and 1968, reaching a trough at about the time of the devaluation of sterling. After 1969 there has been some recovery, partly linked with the effects of group control, and at the time of the study demand for foundry products was very high. Commercial management and foundry managers were worried that delivery delays caused by strikes could alienate the major car manufacturers, who were then having a lot of trouble with suppliers. The narrowness of profit margins and the possible loss of trade had led higher management to put pressure on foundry managers and they in turn on supervisors, to settle disputes on any terms rather than interrupt production. Lower management, naturally more conscious of the problems in their relationships on the shop floor, had been less willing to back down. In consequence, tension had developed inside the managerial hierarchy.

The managerial structure had a preponderance of direct production expertise, with the personnel, work-study and allied departments possessing a subordinate role and little authority. These special departments had been employed in a limited role akin to that described as 'fire fighting' by the Commission on Industrial Relations (CIR) with reference to Birmid Qualcast[11]. In part, the lack of authority in the personnel and work-study departments was the outcome of the traditional independence of the foundry managements, which derived from the period when the foundries were not all controlled by the same company. Foundry managers still felt it was unnecessary to call in experts when they had always handled their own manpower problems. One final point that should be mentioned here is that members of middle management often had a short career at the foundries, compared with senior managers and supervisors. Turnover was high and foundry managers were sometimes forced out unless their results were good. This insecurity bred either apathy or frantic attempts to impress, both of which were detrimental to labour relations. Turnover, however, had not led to the recruitment of managers with no experience of foundry customs. Many of these customs are the same everywhere: all the managers were recruited from the supervisors' grade, and had substantial experience of the industry.

An account of the foundries should include a brief account of union organization at the time of the study. There were three unions. Manual workers were organized either by the Amalgamated Union of Engineering and Foundry Workers (AEF) or the Transport and General Workers Union (TGWU). Foremen and supervisors were organized by the Association of Scientific, Technical and Managerial Staffs (ASTMS). Of these the AEF had been present for the longest period of time, with continuous organization dating back to the post-war years. The TGWU had only organized workers there since 1968, and the most recent arrival was ASTMS. The growth and role of the unions is examined more fully in Chapters 3 and 4.

3

Patterns in Custom and Practice

SUBSTANTIVE REGULATION

Wages and their Determination

Some of the major aspects of the system of wage determination were unilaterally imposed by management. Although the foundries did not belong to the Engineering Employers' Federation, the basis of all hourly rates, hours worked, holidays, and overtime payments, was the National Engineering Agreement[12]. The arrangement was convenient as it saved the company some of the problems of bargaining or making other arrangements to cover these points. Since 1950 the comparatively weak Foundry Workers' Union (which subsequently amalgamated with the Engineers to form the AEF) had not questioned these basic rules. Where output depended upon effort and was easy to measure—as for moulders, casters, dressers, coremakers, knock-out labourers and other occupations and grades—management had imposed schemes of incentive payment which were not related to the National Engineering Agreement. But in many of these schemes, some parts of total earnings were not negotiable since management regarded such components as the cost-of-living bonus given to piece-workers as fixed. (This bonus had remained at a fixed figure of £8 6s 9d for several years and represented a diminishing part of the piece-workers' total earnings.)

One consequence of this arrangement was that over the

years total earnings became progressively more unstable. The cost-of-living bonus was the only stable part of the piece-workers' earnings, and the other components fluctuated widely from week to week and from individual to individual. As the fluctuating components rose, with bargaining being exclusively concentrated upon them, so the instability of total earnings increased. Piece-workers were thus in no position to bargain for a more stable system of payment since the predominance of informal regulation meant there was no machinery, precedent, or encouragement from management to bring it about. Custom-and-practice rules had developed to allow changes in some items of earnings, but the limitations of informal bargaining had left management with complete control over other aspects, and comparatively few areas were covered by joint rules which allowed agreed changes to take place. This limit on flexibility had led both to distortions in the working of the payment system and to the development of potential sources of workers' dissatisfaction. The growing dependence of time-workers upon doing 10 or 20 hours overtime a week, as the national basic rate became increasingly out of touch with average earnings, constituted another example of the effects of limiting the area of bargaining.

Although several crucial areas of wage determination were the prerogative of management, there still existed a number of ways in which the workers could influence the conditions of their work. Obviously, workers on incentive schemes can bargain about piece-rates, whilst for time-workers overtime and merit bonuses become important. These topics were not covered by any collective agreements until very recently, so no formal rules existed to govern behaviour of either workers or management. Custom-and-practice rules filled the gap. Two areas of regulation which are comparatively easy to study are examined here.

These are wage differentials and methods of piece-work bargaining.

There existed an internal system of earnings differentials that was entirely the outcome of informal understandings shared by management and workers, such as regulated the relationship between the earnings of unskilled knock-out men and the moulders with whom they worked. The differentials tended to be ordinal rather than cardinal, in the sense that one group would be happy as long as their earnings exceeded those of another group: the exact size of this difference was less important. Moulders were earning about £35 for 40 hours, which was about £10 more than unskilled earnings for 40 hours; dressers earned £4–5 less than moulders for 40 hours, as did casters and chargers.

Where work-groups were well established these differentials became fairly stable. But certain factors militated against any rigid system of relativities. Reference groups were limited: men would relate their earnings to others in the same shop, but rarely to earnings in other foundries. The extreme fragmentation of the technical processes and of the piece-work payment system meant that large inter-foundry disparities were not uncommon, and heavy earnings fluctuations, due to variable overtime and production stoppages, complicated comparisons. Thus core-makers in one foundry could be earning nearly twice as much as core-makers elsewhere. In addition, a system of differentials depends to a large extent upon the existence of social links between groups for the transfer of information. The existence of different ethnic work-groups obstructed communications, so that comparisons became more difficult. Labour turnover also meant that a fair proportion of workers never learned and accepted the customary differences. Complete stability of earnings differentials also depends on all workers having equal control over methods of increasing earnings and on their unquestioning acceptance of past relativities. At the time of the study, heavy piece-work wage drift, and other de-stabilizing forces some of which depended upon racial factors, had upset the traditional differences, especially between piece-workers and time-workers such as maintenance men. In piece-work bargaining, custom and practice controlled changes : piece-rates were decentralized in the sense that they were settled between the supervisor and the individual, or the group for which they applied. Since some workers such as moulders and casters were paid on a group bonus, the bargains sometimes involved as many as fifteen people, but it was more common for two or three men to take their piece-rate for negotiation to the foreman. Shop-stewards were rarely brought in to help an individual to bargain and, on management's side, work study was a rarity, used only in cases where there was a dispute or a new job. Sometimes piece-rates were literally traditional in the sense that prices fixed several years ago would be remembered by a foreman and applied. Fixed lists did not exist for prices for particular products, and this made the role of the individual bargain all the more important. There were no customary limitations upon the frequency with which prices could be re-negotiated, and sometimes price changes would occur every few months. In other instances prices remained fixed for years.

The successful working of this sort of bargaining depended upon two things. Both lower management and the workers had shared norms of a very crude kind about what constituted a fair bargain. These norms were linked in part to relativities and, in part, to what sort of action was appropriate if agreement could not be reached. If a mutually acceptable piece-rate was not fixed, in the past the worker had only two choices: he would either accept it, or leave the job. This was partly due to the absence of strong unions in the work-place, but it was also the consequence of the traditionally high labour turnover, whereby workers are prepared to behave almost as if employment were casual. It seems likely, however, that certain skilled workers with long service found it easier than most unskilled workers with short service, both to fix acceptable piece-rates with a management which comprised their promoted fellows, and to achieve the output necessary to yield high earnings. Men with only a short record of service would be less integrated into the system and less adept at this highly individual form of bargaining. There are some jobs which are preferable to others in that they involve less heavy work and can yield higher earnings, and workers with long experience of the foundry will be aware of the advantage of choosing these jobs, while workers who are inexperienced in the customs of the foundry will find it difficult to adjust to the prevailing mode of allocating work.

When wage bargaining is carried out in this way, with the relationship between the individual and the supervisor or foundry manager being the most important determinant, the system can be highly disorganized; whatever stability exists will in fact be based almost entirely on regularities in the individual bargaining relationship. When the foundries were studied, wage movements appeared chaotic, with unstable relativities and very high rates of drift in piece-work earnings. The clearest cases of wage drift were among the knock-out labourers in foundry 1, who had increased their earnings by pressure upon piece-rates from about £25 to £35 for 40 hours. Workers on the shot blast had also substantially raised the piece-rate part of their earnings from about 10 per cent of total earnings to 40 per cent of total earnings. Overtime drift was probably more important for many groups, including other knock-out labourers who averaged 20 hours overtime a week in foundry 2, and cupola operators who averaged between 10 and 20 hours overtime a week in foundry 1. It is very difficult to give conclusive evidence of earnings drift in a particular plant unless there are good statistics for a long period, and in this case a great deal of the evidence is indirect rather than based upon an examination of overtime earnings. However, the break-down of stable relativities appears to be of fairly recent origin, and in some areas of employment the old relation-ships were still intact.

Prior to 1968, when the AEF was the only union, individual bargaining seemed to work quite efficiently and was associated with comparative social stability and acceptance by the workers of the norms of wage determi-nation. The signs of collapse mentioned above have occurred since the immigrants developed their own union activity. This is not to say that the unions contributed to the breakdown by initiating competitive claims, such as those which seem to have been behind the collapse of informal bargaining at the Birmid Qualcast group of foundries. At the foundries studied here the unions were rarely involved in piece-work bargaining, or at least they did not formulate claims for piece-rates.

It does not follow that any particular set of factors was responsible for the growing disorder in substantive relation-ships. Only two arguments are being advanced here. First, that custom-and-practice rules dominated the areas of decision-making where workers could influence their earnings. Second, that these rules had two major qualities: they were shared between management and workers, and worked best where consensus existed between the parties upon what sort of bargain was acceptable and what methods of bargaining should be employed. Furthermore, this dependence upon informal relationships and shared under-standings made the whole system very susceptible to the growth of disorder where the consensus broke down. This consensus in turn depended heavily upon the degree of socialization of the workers into the system, and the decentralization of bargaining, which meant that workers bargained with immediate supervisors. Close links existed between the supervisors and the 'influential' workers. Supervisors were almost work-mates, and often had more in common with men on the shop floor than with higher management. Later sections will show the role of immigrant work-groups in breaking down some of the specific shared assumptions which were necessary for the system to work with at least some degree of efficiency.

Overtime distribution

Having discussed the way in which piece-workers controlled their earnings, it is worth looking at the way in which small groups of men on time-rates controlled, or attempted to control, their own earnings. The main group of workers paid by the hour were the maintenance and other ancillary workers, whose output was difficult to relate to effort. Many of these workers were employed in small units and many such groups as storemen, drivers, and night-watchmen had a weak bargaining position in that they could not easily interrupt production to pressurize management. If they wished to increase earnings above the national rates, they had to work overtime. This situation had been reinforced by labour shortages which had led to extremely high overtime levies for all time-workers, but, in particular, for maintenance fitters and electricians. These men got a merit bonus (between £3 and £5 per week) over the national rate, and in every case it was customary for them to come in over weekends, so that they usually worked between 10 and 20 hours overtime a week. Overtime distribution was thus of paramount importance to that 30 per cent of the manual labour force who were exclusively on time-rates. There were some other groups—such as the knock-out sections—for whom the piece-work component was so small that overtime was the main variable element in their earnings.

The operation of overtime distribution may represent another example of the breakdown of a stable system of wage determination where overtime is worked to close a growing gap between national rates and earnings expectations. However, in the foundries the high demand for overtime from the workers led to very little conflict with the management over its allocation. There were several reasons for this. First, high piece-work earnings meant that it was unusual for moulders and well-paid dressers to compete with the less well-paid time-workers and piece-workers for overtime. Secondly, there were customary patterns of allocating particular men to do particular overtime tasks. For instance, knock-out men would work for a few hours cleaning the section of the track where they worked; casters would work on re-lining ladles; and, similarly, much of the routine preparation and cleaning work was allocated on the basis that work was given to the man connected with the job in normal hours. In addition, there was a great deal of productive overtime when management ran some tracks either for an extra hour or for an extra shift. Labour shortages meant that it was often possible for labourers to work two consecutive shifts, or a total of 16 hours, and for some occupations a 12-hour shift was routine. In consequence, overtime was not in short supply and the customary patterns of allocation were not challenged.

The level at which decisions were made was decentralized, with the overtime bargain closely resembling the piece-work bargain. In a sense, high overtime levels sometimes represent disorder in a way that is analogous to the piece-workers' wage drift. Both are signs of the breakdown of managerial control in work-place bargaining. In the foundries studied, the management was not critical of either the high piece-rates or the high overtime, since they thought that they were getting extra work for the higher payments. Probably high overtime was more favoured than high piece-rates, since the output effects were more apparent, but in both cases the suitability of the term 'disorder' was not immediately apparent, at least to management, so that there was little resistance to work-group and individual pressures upon earnings. Management would react to a piece-price demand by saying that a large increase would give the individual 'something to work for'. Similarly, Indians who wanted to work con-secutive shifts were allowed to do so and, frequently, over-time was allowed for maintenance men on the basis that it was customary rather than necessary and because in any case 'there is always work to do'.

However, earnings differentials caused trouble on at least two occasions, and in both cases it was the skilled white workers who were concerned. First, the white maintenance men in foundry 1 became dissatisfied with their differentials and applied an overtime ban for six weeks in the early part of 1970 to try to get a higher basic wage. Regular overtime can create strong dissatisfaction when workers develop expectations of leisure, and this dissatisfaction appears to have developed among the white workers doing regular heavy overtime. Second, between 1966 and 1968, the foundry manager in foundry 1 pursued a policy of reducing labour costs by taking a tough line over piece-rate increases. During this period, the foundry developed by far the lowest average earnings of all, and lost most of its skilled white workers. This turnover was, in a sense, an expression of conflict between management and workers' norms, and derived from the instability of the customary methods of job-regulation in the foundries.

The breakdown of the custom-and-practice rules of the piece-work system and the use of overtime to bolster earnings plainly owe a great deal to general economic factors. Custom is upset by change, and, since the second world war, there has been a progressive tendency for the structure of informal bargaining to create disparities and thus lead to the breakdown of traditional wage and bargaining relationships. This study, however, is not specifically interested in the way in which economic factors contribute to this process, but only in the role of racial factors, and the next sections deal with the areas of custom in which the immigrants contributed most to the breakdown of customary regulation. These are the rules on procedure and on discipline.

PROCEDURAL RULES ON GRIEVANCE HANDLING

Procedural rules involve mutual obligations about the way in which grievances can be legitimately handled. In the absence of conflict over substantive issues, there is no demand for procedural rules. If conflict does arise, then informal rules may involve obligations as binding as written formal rules. The act of writing down a course of action that must be followed when a grievance arises will add nothing to the working of a well-tried set of informal practices that are efficient and mutually acceptable. Very roughly, if both sides are prepared to discuss a grievance in good faith, there is a certain logic in the stages of work-place procedure. This logic derives from the managerial structure, and the advantage of an informal procedure is that it adapts very easily to the realities of both managerial and work-group power.

The procedure at the foundries was informal. There were no formal collective agreements between management and unions to govern the handling of disputes, just as there were no collective agreements on wages until very recently. How-

c

ever, prior to the unionization of the immigrants in 1968, there existed a set of informal understandings between management and the AEF which worked quite well. Moreover, there was little conflict in the foundries over substantive items, and hence little pressure upon the procedure. Such issues as did arise went through an informal process of discussion. Grievances were first raised with the immediate supervisor, who had the authority to settle most shop-floor problems. If there was a failure to agree, the worker was able to consult his shop-steward and then take the issue to the foundry manager. The usual outcome of a failure to agree at this stage was either that the personnel manager and union district official would be called in, or that the issue would be dropped if the union did not feel strongly about it.

Before the immigrants were organized by the Transport and General Workers' Union, the management could rely upon the shop-stewards to follow this procedure for two reasons. First, there existed a genuine sense of obligation amongst the AEF stewards not to strike unless all means of avoiding sanctions had been tried. Secondly, there were occasions when the AEF was quiescent over real abuses of managerial power, and allowed management to impose poor piece-rates or to take other actions that could have been legitimately opposed.

In effect, trade unionism was weak in the foundries, in spite of the fact that the AEF organized many of the skilled workers and nearly half of the total manual labour force. However, this fact must be seen against a background where very few substantive grievances arose, and where those that did were often outside the self-imposed scope of the union. The involvement of the AEF in wage-bargaining or in the protection of custom and practice was intermittent, and action was generally taken in support of those workers who least needed union assistance. This reinforced adherence to voluntary informal norms about the way in which grievances should be processed. Underlying a great deal of this consensus about procedural relations, therefore, was a large measure of agreement with the most importal levels of management on what were 'fair' substantive settlements. The interrelation between the two facets of job regulation is important in explaining the comparative success of the informal procedures.

Another important element in the working of the procedures was the relationship between shop-stewards and management. Shop-stewards can contribute more to the viability of procedures than anyone else. It is difficult to generalize about the AEF stewards, partly because there had been substantial turnover, but the most influential of them, a convenor and branch secretary, had been in employment at the foundries for nearly twenty years, and had developed both control over shop-stewards and members and influence over all the important managers. His personal views upon what constituted justifiable behaviour exerted considerable pressure, and his personal stability had contributed to the survival of the informal procedures. He represented the element of craft exclusiveness in the union, restricting membership to the workers with the fewest grievances—the well-paid piece-workers and the craftsmen. Only recently had the erosion of differentials created dissatisfaction in the ranks of the AEF.

At this stage there will be no examination of what went wrong with the procedures, since the collapse of customs in this area was due almost entirely to the immigrant work-units, and needs to be seen in the light of an understanding of how these work-units operated.

DISCIPLINARY RULES

The tradition of unilateral regulation by the employer

hangs heavily over disciplinary rules, not least in the foundry industry. Disciplinary rules in the foundries studied operated in much the same way as other substantive and procedural rules, with the lowest levels of management having discretionary authority. All supervisors had the power to dismiss men without giving reasons. There were no prescribed penalties for particular offences, and managerial discretion often favoured severity. Dismissals were quite frequent. This crude system depended upon the consent of both parties and, in practice, the approval of the union was due to the fact that, in most cases, the AEF members were well enough acquainted with the system to avoid trouble. There seems to have been wide managerial leeway over offences such as swearing at a supervisor, lengthening breaks, and absence from work, so that knowledge of where management would draw the line depended on experience, and thus upon socialization into the prevailing norms of the work-place. The AEF did not appear to have been involved in disputes over discipline during the previous few years. This fact reinforces the view that the AEF shared managerial norms about job-regulation, and was also reluctant to take action where there were genuine abuses. The attitudes of conformity among the AEF shop-stewards meant that the union offered an inadequate focus for resistance to particular disciplinary abuses or managerial practices.

THE AEF: ITS GROWTH AND ROLE IN THE SYSTEM

The Foundry Workers' Union began to organize workers in the skilled grades in the late 1940s, and over a period of several years succeeded in recruiting about 50 per cent of the manual labour force. The rate of unionization was fairly slow, and in no cases did whole shops or sections become imbued with strong union consciousness. Recruitment took place mainly through the branch rather than through the shop-stewards, and the act of joining in this way tends to require stronger individual motivation than if a whole shop becomes unionized in a rapid burst of growth. This pattern of growth is not uncommon among craft unions, and also characterized the growth of the AEF in the Birmingham tool-rooms.

There appears to be a strong connection between this style of growth and the prevalence of individual bargaining, since both the foundries studied and the Birmingham tool-rooms were characterized until recently by extreme fragmentation of payment systems, with earnings depending upon individual skill and status. Individual bargaining does not provide a basis for a strong workshop organization. The fragmentation of the payments systems and the élitist nature of the AEF membership meant that the union was actually very little involved in wage negotiation, and the absence of a 'standard rate' undermined the development of social cohesion on the shop floor. This tallies with the traditional sources of solidarity in craft unions, which have tended to be centred on the control of labour supply, manning and work practices. The individual looks to the union to secure these aspects of his work situation, while relying upon his personal bargaining power to safeguard differentials.

In the foundries studied, the AEF followed this pattern, with the union being most concerned about what could be called the 'craft custom and practice' of foundry work. But foundry work provides a weaker basis than some other industries for traditional 'craft custom and practice', since the apprentice system is long defunct, with the erosion of skilled hand-moulding. The custom-and-practice rules which remain depend on the absence of challenge from management or other workers. Since there was little bargaining, and that was mainly conducted by the individual or the small group, the union played a relatively unimportant role. Its growth did not upset the pattern of relationships which had existed before, and it was not a source of effective power and influence.

There are, however, one or two exceptions to this generalization, and they must be mentioned to try and put the role of the union in perspective. Closed shops developed in the maintenance shops, and the union controlled entry, work assignment, shift working and sometimes the administration of merit bonuses in these shops. Elsewhere the union exerted some influence over the piece-work system. For instance, on the few tracks with group piece-rates, a shop-steward would take the lead in negotiations.

Perhaps the best way in which the AEF's function can be understood is to compare them with what Turner[13] sees as one of the central characteristics of the early cotton unions. Turner shows that the hand-weavers' unions had their origins in conventional social relations and, for decades, these early cotton unions only intermittently developed beyond informal work-group organizations. The basic motives or policies of the unions thus differed very little from the informal work-group aims. Similarly there was little difference between the role of the union and that of the informal work-groups in the foundries. Regulation was hardly carried beyond what was normally done by the workers before they joined the union.

Initially, the AEF, as the only union in the foundries, recruited all grades of worker but tended to concentrate on those who were already socialized into the foundry culture—the skilled production-workers and maintenance men. The branch had no policy of discrimination or restriction of numbers, possibly because there was no strong independent pressure from immigrants to join the union. Such immigrants as did join the AEF were usually employed in the occupations that the union had organized well, notably maintenance and moulding, but it was unusual for immigrants to enter these occupations. In foundry 1b, for a period, one AEF shop-steward refused to recruit immigrants, and managed to keep his section of the union from having any coloured members. The other stewards appear to have accepted any immigrants who wished to join, but did not go out of their way to encourage membership.

4
Ethnic Work-Units

THE CONCEPT

A great deal has been written recently about the operation of informal regulation in British industry, and, in consequence, much of what has been said so far does not constitute fresh analysis, although it shows how such rules work in the specific context of the foundry industry. In contrast, virtually nothing has been written about the way that ethnic work-groups or gangs operate, or about their special characteristics.

In this context the expression 'ethnic work-group' is used to refer to a situation where an extreme form of segregation exists in the work-place. Plainly such a situation can contain several elements, not all of which are necessary ones. Slavery can be maintained by legal authority: in the foundries studied, legal authority would obviously not be one of the elements perpetuating separation. The two major elements present were a language barrier, and linked to this, various social predispositions towards separation.

The existence of a language barrier would necessarily lead to the development of a particular form of organization among immigrants. The majority of immigrants in these foundries were Punjabis, who could not speak English and who therefore had to take instruction from fellow-workers who were bi-lingual. In the Southall case[14] also, the majority of the immigrants were Punjabis who could not speak English. The importance of the language barrier is that non-English-speaking immigrants develop patterns of social interaction at work which effectively prevent absorption and the development of social relations with white workers. The immigrant gains employment through a contact in his community, learns his job from a go-between, and, where the work necessitates contact with other workers, he is generally restricted to working with fellow countrymen. The work will tend to be unskilled, to remove the need for training off the job, and where this is allied to intrinsically unpleasant work, the development of the ethnic work-group will be encouraged by certain dispositions of white workers and management. White workers will rarely compete for such jobs, especially in a tight labour market, and they will be driven from the particular occupation by virtue of their own high turnover. Management, faced with a labour shortage, responds by encouraging the employment of non-English-speaking immigrants. We see, therefore, that not only are there powerful tendencies for such immigrants to gather in occupational groups, but that these social forces can be reinforced by the attitutudes of members of the host society.

Where a language barrier exists, social forces relating to the needs of both the immigrants and the host society will force the immigrants into effectively self-contained groups. However, ethnic work-groups can also develop in the absence of a language barrier. Where race is linked to social stratification then racial occupations may develop. West Indians may find acculturation easier than Indians and Pakistanis because English is their native language, but lack of industrial skills may nevertheless limit their choice of employment to occupations dominated by other unskilled immigrants. In this sort of case, the self-reinforcing tendencies towards segregation in employment, though weak, will still be present.

Several factors have been mentioned that can lead to the

reduction of inter-racial contact at work. These factors—
legal authority, language, stratification factors and social
attitudes—may lead to different forms of ethnic work-
group, with different relationships between the ethnic
group, the employer and other groups such as white
workers. Many factors can impinge upon the 'shape' and
characteristics of an ethnic work-unit. The evidence on the
foundries included in the following section relates to one
possible form of ethnic work-group. In this case the
language barrier and a variety of technical, labour-market
and attitudinal factors were of primary importance.

EVIDENCE OF ETHNIC WORK-GROUPS IN THE FOUNDRIES

The four foundries employed a total labour force of about
950 workers, including supervisory, technical, clerical and
managerial staffs; of these, 802 were manual workers. It
would have been useful to calculate both the proportion of
immigrants in employment, and the rate of build-up to this
level. Unfortunately a detailed picture of the rate of build-
up of immigrants could not be calculated owing to deficient
records. It is relatively simple to work out the overall proportions of immigrants to white workers and the proportions
in each foundry, but this does not reveal very much about
the degree of integration of immigrants into the labour
force. A certain amount of segregation appears from the
analysis of different skill categories. Some grades of skill are
dominated by white workers and others by coloured
workers. Occupational analysis brings another dimension
of poor integration into view. Not only is there a tendency
towards segregation by skill, but also particular occupations
appear to be mostly staffed by immigrants. The examination of the composition and siting of work-groups on the
shop floor adds a further dimension to the study of

segregation inside occupations. Finally, another indicator of integration of immigrants into the work force is the extent to which the unions are integrated. If the distribution of immigrants by skill, occupation, work-group and trade union is analysed, then a fairly complete picture of social and work relationships inside the foundry will emerge.

Skill Classification

For analysis of labour statistics, foundries 1a and 1b have been added together, and contrasted with foundries 2 and 3. Manual workers were classified into skilled, semi-skilled and unskilled groups by foundry, and then the proportion of immigrants in these groups was calculated.

TABLE 1: *ANALYSIS OF THE LABOUR FORCE BY SKILL*

	Foundry 1	Foundry 2	Foundry 3	Overall
Immigrants as a percentage of the skilled workers	39%	11%	41%	30%
Immigrants as a percentage of the semi-skilled	34%	50%	62%	49%
Immigrants as a percentage of the unskilled	48%	58%	62%	58%
Immigrants as a percentage of the total labour	41%	35%	54%	52%

In terms of skill classifications, it can be seen from Table 1 that there was a tendency for immigrants to be concentrated in unskilled or semi-skilled work, while white workers were proportionately more numerous in skilled work. This might be taken as a sign that white workers tend to have higher status, or that, when promotion opportunities arise, the immigrants, being new arrivals, do not have sufficient seniority to gain skilled jobs. But there are several reasons why these simple conclusions cannot be accepted.

First, there were significant differences between the

foundries, with foundry 1 immigrants distributed fairly evenly between skilled and unskilled work, and foundry 2 at the other extreme. In addition, foundry 3 had a very high overall proportion of immigrants, so that although no more skilled workers were immigrants than in foundry 1, there were more coloured unskilled and semi-skilled workers. These variations between foundries were due to a noticeable deficiency of skilled immigrants at foundry 2 and an unusually high proportion of unskilled immigrants at foundry 3. It is difficult to draw any conclusions about integration or differential status from these figures, but it is worth noting that foundry 1 had by far the highest turnover in all grades, and this had opened the skilled grades to immigrant entry. Hence the even distribution of immigrants by skill.

Secondly, all foundry work, with the borderline exceptions of maintenance and a little moulding, is basically repetitive, semi-skilled work. The demise of hand-moulding has eroded the genuine craft work, and now skills essentially consist of dexterity and experience. There are good moulders and bad ones, but the difference is one of a few months' practice on the job, not a long apprenticeship. A lot of workers are thus classified as skilled simply because of the traditional status of their job. In addition many semi-skilled workers do not (properly speaking) possess any skill at all, but have been promoted to give them a higher time-rate. Instances are the warehousemen, sand-blast workers and core-conveyors. Unskilled workers generally fall into three classes. Some are women, in inherently simple jobs such as cleaning toilets, others are night watchmen, and still others are on piece-rates so that the classification has little effect on their earnings. No meaningful conclusion can be drawn about either the status of immigrants or the segregation of coloured workers in unskilled work from the classification of skill used in the foundries.

TABLE 2: *OCCUPATIONAL ANALYSIS OF THE LABOUR FORCE*

Occupation: skilled	Foundry 1			Foundry 2			Foundry 3		
	White male	Coloured male	Female*	White male	Coloured male	Female	White male	Coloured male	Female
Caster	8	6		9	2		9	5	
Cupola operator	7	13		15			1	1	
Crane-drive cupola operator	—	—		1	—		3	—	
Furnace-man	1	2		—	—		—	1	
Moulder	43	31		60	—		21	5	
Pattern-maker	8	—		5	—		4	—	
Dresser	9	15		10	10	1	2	18	
Maintenance worker	28	—		17	3		8	5	
Sub-total:	98	67	—	116	15	1	49	35	—
Occupation: semi-skilled									
Checker	1	4		—	3		1	—	
Clamp worker	2	—		—	—		1	6	
Fettler	4	2		2	—		2	—	
Sand-blast operator	2	7		1	7		1	—	
Shot-blast operator	1	2		—	7		—	13	
Van-driver	7	1		6	4		2	—	
Warehouseman	11	1		7	2		2	—	
Inspector	11	—		8	3	3	4	—	
Works policeman	3	—		3	—		3	—	
Painter	1	1		2	—		1	2	
Grinder	1	6		—	12		—	9	
Core-conveyor	1	—		—	—		1	1	
Crane-driver	2	—		—	2		1	—	
Sub-total:	45	24	—	39	40	3	19	31	—

TABLE 2 continued

Occupation: unskilled	Foundry 1			Foundry 2			Foundry 3		
	White male	Coloured male	Female*	White male	Coloured male	Female	White male	Coloured male	Female
Core-maker	9	21	19	14	1	9	4	6	2
General labourer	4	10	—	1	19	—	2	7	—
Knock-out labourer	4	23		2	20		—	11	—
Night watchman	—	—		—	—		1	—	
Toilet cleaner	1	1		—	—		2	—	
Basket Bobber/Sorter	—	—	10	—	4	5	—	6	3
Cleaner			6			1			—
Central services mechanic	10								
Sub-total:	28	56	35	17	44	15	9	30	5
TOTAL:	171	147	40	162	99	19	77	96	5

*There were no coloured females.

Occupational Classification

By contrast, the occupational classification reveals a striking tendency to segregation. By looking at the more numerous grades in Table 2, such as moulders, dressers, maintenance and knock-out men, it can be seen that there were instances where one race monopolized a job. At foundry 2, there were no coloured moulders, but 60 white moulders, while there were 54 immigrant knock-out men in all the foundries, compared with 6 white men. At foundries 1 and 2, dressers were well mixed, but at foundry 3 there were only 2 white dressers, as opposed to 18 immigrants. Given some inter-foundry differences, there were substantial pockets of segregation, though the term 'segregation' is used guardedly and does not refer to a deliberate policy.

There was a strong tendency for direct production workers to be immigrants (except for moulders and skilled grades) while ancillary grades were nearly always either white or West Indian. This indicates one of the patterns of separation. Immigrants were most numerous in simple direct production jobs, which are easily controlled and require few instructions; and they were concentrated in comparatively few occupations. At foundry 3, there were immigrants in 15 out of 28 occupational categories, while white workers were in 23 of them. This can be explained by language barriers, since those immigrants who do not work in large groups tend to be the few who can speak English; otherwise they have to work close to a worker who is bilingual.

While the occupational analysis reveals that some occupations were not integrated, in the sense that both immigrants and white workers tend to do different jobs, there were many cases of apparent integration, such as casting, core-making, van-driving and, in two foundries, dressing. But occupational breakdown, like the skill classification, is a misleading guide. While an occupation may appear to be integrated in overall figures, separation may occur at individual foundries. This was the case with dressing and core-making. At foundry 2, there was only one immigrant on core-making, in spite of the fact that at the other foundries, the job was dominated by white females (there were no immigrant females) and coloured youths. There was a tradition of employing females on core-making, and they tended to be a depressed class in terms of earnings, and had adopted militant attitudes, some of them joining the same union as the immigrants.

Work-Group Classification

The other reason that the occupational analysis does not give a true measure of segregation is that work-groups do not conform to the occupational breakdown. In foundry 1a, the apparently integrated moulders in fact consisted of immigrants working on one track while white workers were on the other. The same was true of the dressers at foundries 1 and 2, since they belonged to ethnic gangs. It is worth remembering that some of these large occupations were paid on group incentives, and I did not come across immigrants and white workers in the same payment group. Other cases of this sort of separation were the immigrant fitters and maintenance men in foundries 2 and 3, all of whom worked on the night shift when they were, for the most part, working amongst other immigrants. Casters did not work in groups, but they were usually attached to groups of their own race. Thus, in spite of first appearances, the reality revealed by the work-group distribution was that there were comparatively few immigrants who were well integrated in their working lives. Most of them worked in gangs on direct production occupations and had little work contact with white workers.

The concept of a work-group only acquires meaning in a specific context, or where the nature of the group activity is defined. Work-groups can arise where people work in the same area, or have breaks together, or bargain together, or engage collectively in other patterns of social behaviour. For bargaining purposes, and with respect to the organization of work, the immigrants tended to have minimal contact with white workers. In addition, it appeared that other social contacts were based largely on work contacts, and lunch groups and other social groups were, in practice, segregated.

Union Membership Classification

Union membership is the one form of social interaction

which revealed a marginal tendency to absorption. A union can provide an integrating force even when the usual work situation is divisive. Joint union action can be a basis for social relations which cut across work-groups and occupations. Beryl Radin noted some cases where integration was strengthened by immigrants coming out on strike in support of white workers[15]. Moreover, if there is no closed shop, then the choice between unions can indicate genuine social preferences and trends in group cohesion that cannot be easily tested in other ways.

The TGWU had recruited no white workers at the foundries. The AEF, however, had pockets of immigrant membership varying by occupation and foundry. Foundry 3 had the most immigrants in the AEF, with a fairly open recruitment policy bringing in a whole section of dressers who transferred from the TGWU. There were, in addition, the immigrant maintenance workers in foundries 2 and 3 who were entirely organized by the AEF, which operated an informal closed shop. As with the other indicators, there were substantial differences between the foundries. Foundry 1 was characterized by a complete membership split by colour. In foundry 2 there were only half a dozen immigrants in the AEF, and these were covered by informal closed-shop agreements. Foundry 3 had a rather more fluid situation, with transfers, some poaching, and a few inter-union disputes over membership, indicating that racial factors were less important than occupational ones in determining union membership. Trends in membership had been for immigrants to leave the AEF as the TGWU developed, and polarization became more extreme, with the possible exception of foundry 3 where the racial situation was more complex. There the presence of a Pakistani senior steward in the TGWU alienated some Indians and, in addition, weakened the racial cohesion uniting the immigrants elsewhere, so that workers responded to occupational factors in choosing a union.

In general, it appears that the racial distribution of union membership reinforces the tendency towards separation rather than providing an integrative mechanism. But this conclusion was not wholly true of foundry 3, which also had other distinctive features. It had a record of industrial peace, the only recorded disputes being over union membership, and these disputes were settled in the procedure before any action was taken.

The preceding analysis of the labour force has shown that in spite of the employment of a large number of immigrants in the foundries there was little evidence of integration. But there are several other aspects to the operation of ethnic work-units, other than mere separation, which must be examined. First, it is interesting to see the extent to which the immigrants themselves were ethnically uniform, and how exceptions to that pattern affected relationships. Secondly, the extent to which the immigrants could speak English has to be looked at. Thirdly, attention must be given to the way in which these groups grew and recruited other immigrants, while excluding white workers. Fourthly, the role of bi-lingual intermediaries is important.

THE OPERATION OF ETHNIC WORK-UNITS

There were some interesting variations in the origin of the immigrants in employment at the foundries. Of 342 immigrant males, about 60 were Pakistanis, about 10 were West Indians, and the rest were Indian Punjabis. For most purposes the West Indians could be classed with the white workers, since they showed no tendency towards racial solidarity and often worked with white men in ancillary task such as driving or working in the stores. The Pakistanis were not concentrated and seemed to mix well with the Indians. Though the Pakistani senior steward was isolated on the shop-stewards' committee, the basis of his support was Indian. Racial solidarity does not mean unanimity on every subject, and there were Indian factions, though these were unconnected with the Indian Workers' Association, which apparently helped to cause internal political conflict at Birmid Qualcast[16]. There were splits upon policy amongst the Indians, with the younger and more radical shop-stewards in foundry 1 coming into conflict with the older ones at foundry 2. There was also some attempted blacklegging during strikes, and some of the immigrants had not joined the union even after the danger of victimization had been removed. The Southall study showed some of the ways in which disunity can occur amongst immigrant workers, and several of the factors were operative in these foundries.

Research difficulties made it impossible to test the extent to which the immigrants could speak English. It was obvious, however, that few could speak English fluently, and even some of the shop-stewards could not converse in English. It seems likely that most of the shop-stewards were chosen on the basis that they could talk to the management. But at foundries 1 and 3 these men were not the natural leaders of the community, and this created problems of communication in bargaining. At foundry 2, however, the senior steward was important in the community, and his voice carried considerable authority. The immigrants who could speak English were often to be found in jobs either where they worked alongside white workers or where they could act as communicators between the supervisors and ethnic groups. There were no coloured supervisors.

Fluency is difficult to measure, since supervisors and immigrants often found ways of communicating without properly learning the other's language. The use of key terms can help in some situations. Immigrants with long service in the foundry had generally acquired enough English to get along, and thus turnover rates were vital in determining this aspect of integration. At foundry 3, where integration was most advanced in terms of work-groups and union membership, there was a large stable core of Indians and Pakistanis with several years' service. At foundry I the turn-over rate was very much higher for all workers, and many new entrants appeared to be recent immigrants with no fluency in English.

Out of the language barrier develops the role of the go-between, the strength of the shop-steward, and the recruit-ing practices that effectively form these work-groups. The official method of recruitment was for the personnel department to notify vacancies to the local Employment Exchange. In fact, the only vacancies that were notified were those for particular specialists such as laboratory or clerical staff. The tradition of foundry independence meant that foundry managers recruited their own manual workers. The only vacancies that they notified to the personnel department were for skilled workers such as fitters who were in short supply. However, the practice of internal promotion to most skilled jobs meant that most vacancies were for women and unskilled labour. When particular shortages arose, the immigrants usually notified friends or relations, who applied to the foundry managers. Thus a large proportion of the intake had settled social relationships before they started and did not need to learn English either to get employment or to continue in it. The influence of the extended family upon this form of recruit-ment meant that the work-groups were often united by strong cohesive forces which were not present among white workers. As a matter of interest, there was no indication of bribery of supervisors to get work, as has happened else-where, but such arrangements are necessarily secret. There was no evidence of attempts to exclude white workers from working in otherwise solid ethnic groups, and white men were taken on, for instance in knock-out sections, but they generally left. The structure of this sort of group ossifies relationships and makes integration impossible since white men are often unwilling to work in groups where the prevailing norms and behaviour are not English. When the study was carried out, the Midlands suffered from real labour shortages and the local Employment Exchange recorded an unemployment rate of under 1 per cent, so other work in more congenial surroundings was often available.

Another characteristic of ethnic work-units is that the traditional customs of the immigrants remain undiluted since there are no forces acting to break them down inside the group. Language is only the most obvious of the barriers. Customary views of morality, discipline, seniority in promotion, work behaviour and social ties and responsibilities also govern work-group behaviour. For instance, men from a largely agricultural background have no tradition of limiting output. The view of what constitutes an offence worthy of dismissal essentially derives from a society in which dismissal often entails cutting off family and social ties. Work-group norms on promotion derive from the pre-industrial social structure of the village communities from which the immigrants came. Long working hours are traditional, so that twelve-hour shifts are acceptable to immigrants. In an agricultural community lateness and absenteeism are not regarded as real misdemeanours. Perhaps these examples are enough to show not only the different norms that immigrants possess, but also the possibilities of conflict with management and white workers when these traditions are safeguarded inside the ethnic work-units. A heavy responsibility devolves upon the group leaders, since they may have to explain such things as the customs of the foundry, the payment system, and the works rules. Considerable confusion can arise if the workers do not understand them properly.

In looking at the operation of ethnic work-units, it is

D*

worth bringing in some of the more general aspects of the labour situation, and, in particular, labour turnover. The overall turnover rate was very high, approaching 50 per cent per annum. However, this instability was localized, and the 50 per cent rate did not apply to all groups in all foundries. To begin with there was a stable core in the labour force. This was very largely composed of white skilled workers, such as moulders, and large parts of the AEF membership had very long records of service. There were, however, other areas of stability, notably the women core-makers and, increasingly, the immigrants. In particular, turnover varied from foundry to foundry, with foundry 1 having a very high rate among all the workers and foundry 3 having a stable force. This was related to earnings, which were highest at foundry 3, but other factors such as managerial behaviour and immigrant integration were probably also important. It is not easy to draw further conclusions, simply because the records were a poor basis for generalization, but the impact of turnover at foundry 1 was plainly very important in creating a labour force which was not adjusted to the custom-and-practice rules of the foundry. It appears, also, that the stability of white skilled groups generally meant that a conservative force existed which was prepared to defend custom and which created the continuity essential for custom to survive.

When a worker enters a particular work culture there is always an induction crisis, in which he either adjusts to the situation, or decides to leave. It is in this period that turnover is generally highest. Immigrants entering the foundries to do unskilled work experienced an induction crisis which was prolonged by the cushioning of the ethnic work-groups. The high turnover rate shows that many of them were not staying long enough to make the transition and become absorbed by the factory's traditional culture. Turnover statistics need to be sophisticated to yield any useful results, and in this case they were not adequate to show exactly which groups had the greatest turnover rates, or the size of the stable and unstable proportions. Besides, race and earnings were certainly not the only important influences on turnover. Unpleasant conditions and a low proportion of genuinely skilled jobs provided additional motives for leaving employment.

If the pool of labour on which they draw is large enough turnover may not substantially affect the working of ethnic groups. These foundries were comparatively small, but recruited from the whole of the Birmingham area, and, in consequence, turnover does not appear to have led to the breakdown of any groups. Indeed the immigrant work-groups appear to have been most cohesive in foundry 1 where turnover was highest partly perhaps because of their greater sense of insecurity regarding work rights. But turn-over—though not disrupting groups—does appear to have influenced their behaviour considerably.

UNION ORGANIZATION OF IMMIGRANTS

Between 1968 and 1970, another union developed in the foundries to rival the AEF. In mid–1968, the immigrants at foundry 2 joined the TGWU, and early in 1969 the union began to organize in foundry 3. Later that year, they tried to organize foundry 1b, but failed, and only in 1970 did a continuous organization take root there. Immigrants at foundry 1a remain as yet unorganized, with the exception of six men and a shop-steward, who have no substantial following.

This pattern of growth provides several contrasts with that of the AEF. Instead of membership developing slowly on the basis of individual motivation, strong work-group norms developed and hastened the rate of growth. Such a

pattern of growth, where whole shops become unionized, is
not unusual, but it demonstrates a cohesion that was not
evident among the white workers, and provides the basis
for a strong shop-floor organization. The present levels of
membership were reached within weeks. In foundry 1,
about 75 immigrants were in the TGWU, comprising about
51 per cent of the immigrants. One of the reasons for this
low overall figure was the absence of an organization in
foundry 1a. In foundry 2, there were 95 members, comprising about 95 per cent of the immigrants. At foundry 3,
there were 61 members, or 62 per cent of the immigrants.
With the exception of foundry 1, nearly all workers
irrespective of colour were in one or other of the unions, so
these figures provide an indicator of the group cohesion of
the immigrants.

The union organization drives involved secret meetings
at local halls. Indians with trade-union experience insti-
gated the process at foundry 2, and the others emulated it
both in joining the TGWU and in holding secret meetings.
At foundry 1, the first meeting was discovered and the
leaders dismissed, but members were recruited later and
management only discovered the organization when they
tried to make a community leader redundant. (Subsequently he became senior shop steward for all the
foundries.) Management resisted the union on the grounds
that the AEF could cater for anyone with an inclination to
join a union, and apparently refused initially to recognize
the stewards. However, stoppages at foundries 1 and 2 led
to recognition of the union's right to bargain over some
topics, though the extent of recognition was never clear.

Generally full-time officers of the TGWU were little
involved in plant affairs, unless disputes occurred and they
were called in to help achieve a settlement. One of the consequences of the rapid informal growth of the plant organization, with weak connections with the district, was that

there was little initial contact between the district organizers and the shop-stewards. The officials only discovered the foundry organization when initial disputes in the plants got out of hand, and in some cases were unaware that they had members in particular foundries. The shop-stewards received no training, or assistance, except when strikes occurred. Consequently at the beginning the immigrants had no guidance from experienced white officials in handling the problems of securing an established place for a new and rapidly developed union inside the traditional framework of industrial relations. Nor do the immigrants seem to have had clear-cut objectives in turning to the TGWU. The influx into the union appears to have been a consequence of a strong communal instinct or feeling rather than an outcome of specific grievances or general demands. In foundries 1 and 3, there was, in addition, a strong element of imitation of the successful example of foundry 2, where the behaviour pattern was set.

However, while the immigrants had no conscious intention of changing the system of industrial relations in the foundries, it seems that the factors which influenced union growth had implications for the informal fragmented system of bargaining. Growth was an indirect consequence of the cohesion of the immigrants' ethnic work-units, and these work-units were the basis of union organization, with shop stewards being elected for most of them. Group solidarity of this sort produced tensions in the existing system of individual fragmented bargaining and created demands for group standards. Examples of the demand for group bargaining can easily be found in the foundries and, while some were related to wage bargaining, perhaps the most important demands concerned the grievance and disciplinary machinery. The TGWU was an important factor in the development of group wage levels in moulding, dressing and the knock-out sections, and at foundry 3

minimum wage levels were recently agreed at a fairly high
rate for a basic 40-hour week. The knock-out section in
foundry 1 is now paid a regular high basic wage, with a
fall-back rate to minimize fluctuations. Moulders at
foundry 1 and dressers get a guaranteed rate of £35, which
is in part due to TGWU pressure. However, the most
important minimum wage demands in the foundries come
not from the TGWU, surprisingly, but from the AEF,
which has recently become more militant and cohesive. The
AEF shop-stewards put in a claim for a £25 minimum
wage for all occupations in the foundries. In part the AEF's
demands were a response to the TGWU pushfulness. However, the full ramifications of these events need to be seen
in the context of the period of strikes and disorder, which
reinforced group solidarity and led to the polarization of
the various factions in unions and management. The way in
which job regulation developed will therefore become
clearer when the disputes are discussed.

5
Patterns in Industrial Conflict

THE GENERAL NATURE OF CONFLICT IN THE FOUNDRIES

Conflict in the foundries can be classed under four headings. First, there were strikes. These are comparatively easy to study, involving as they did a very noticeable expression of conflict. Secondly, there were disputes which were resolved by means of informal procedures. These disputes are more difficult to study because, owing to the informality of procedure, there are no records to assist systematic examination. Thirdly, there were output restrictions, and small-scale overtime bans. Some of these minor individual expressions of disorder may be recorded, but go-slows and overtime bans generally attract attention only when they are on such a large scale that they are comparable with strikes as 'remarkable' social event. Finally, there was the evidence of turnover and absenteeism rates, which may or may not indicate conflict.

Other methods of classifying conflict are by cause and by the number and types or workers involved. At the foundries, wage disputes can be distinguished from disputes about discipline, procedures and manning, and the disputes involving the TGWU can be separated from those involving the AEF and the ASTMS. It is sometimes useful to classify strikes by the outcome—either in terms of the party that surrenders, or in terms of the way in which a settlement is reached, but only two of the serious strikes at the foundries required a formal settlement before the men returned to work, since most ended independently of any bargaining. It is usual to classify strikes as constitutional or unconstitutional, and to distinguish official from unofficial stoppages, but these distinctions are not very useful for the foundries since all the sanctions were unofficial, and the term 'unconstitutional' does not mean much where there are no codified procedures, although it may be used by either side as a recrimination. In addition, there are differences between the foundries which complicate the problem of analysing causes. Foundry 1 was free from strikes and other forms of disorder until 1970, but it developed a considerable record of unrest after the TGWU began to organize there; foundry 2 has had intermittent disputes over various issues; and foundry 3 has had no unrest at all other than a little inter-union conflict, which was settled by informal discussions.

All the disputes are listed chronologically in Table 3, with details of the causes, the union, the number of men involved, the form of sanction taken (if any), and the way in which a settlement was brought about. Disputes which were settled before any sanctions were resorted to are included to broaden the sample.

Table 3 lists 8 strikes, 2 overtime bans, and 2 go-slows (one of them involving a large number of small go-slows). These were all unofficial; in addition four disputes were settled by discussion. Probably many more disputes were settled by informal procedure, and there may have been other overtime bans and go-slows, but they cannot be traced. Out of the total of 16 cases, 11 involved the TGWU, four involved the AEF, and one involved the ASTMS. This shows the preponderance of the immigrants in the record of disputes. There were three piece-rate disputes, and one dispute over a basic rate, none of them leading to a strike. Five disputes were over suspensions or dismissals, one dispute was over

TABLE 3 : ANALYSIS OF DISPUTES 1969–70

Date and Duration	Foundry/ shop	No. of workers	Type of sanction	Union involved	Status	Reason for dispute	Settlement
(1) 1969 June 6 days	2 foundry: dressers	10	Overtime ban	TGWU	Un-official	Group piece-rate	Increase given
(2) 1970 Jan. 2 days	2 foundry: dressers	4	Go slow	TGWU	Un-official	Piece-rate on product	Provisional settlement while job was timed. One man was dismissed
(3) Jan. 1 day	2 foundry: dressers and foundry labour	50	Strike	TGWU	Un-official	Protest at dismissal in breach of procedure	Dismissal upheld

Table 3—*continued*

Date and Duration	Foundry/ Shop	No. of workers	Type of sanction	Union involved	Status	Reason for dispute	Settlement
(4) March 6th 2 hours	1b foundry: except core shop	35	Sit-down strike	TGWU	Un-official	(a) Redund-ancy of dresser with high status (b) Recogni-tion	Man re-instated Granted
(5) March 14th 2 days	All 1b foundry	45	Strike	TGWU	Un-official	The transfer of work from 1b to 1a dressing shop at the time of re-dundancy in 1a foundry	No action taken to meet demands.

(6) March 17th 2 hours	All 1 foundry	80	Strike	AEF	Un-official	Demand that the TGWU shop stewards be dismissed	No discussions or effort by management to meet demands
(7) April 6th 2 weeks	All 1 foundry	70	Strike	TGWU	Un-official	Dismissal of man for swearing at supervisor and of friends who walked out in sympathy	All reinstated, after long struggle
(8) April 23rd 1 day	Supervisors in all foundries		Strike	ASTMS	Un-official	Protest against the reinstatement of dismissed men	No effect upon management
(9) April 24th 1 day	1 foundry	100	Strike	AEF	Un-official	Protest against re-instatement	No effect

Table 3—continued

Date and Duration	Foundry/ Shop	No. of workers	Type of sanction	Union involved	Status	Reason for dispute	Settlement
May 10th (10)	1 foundry	—	Dispute was settled by discussion	TGWU	—	Promotion of a man to job of caster, caused threat of strike	Management accepted the TGWU candidate
All May (11)	1 foundry: maintenance shop	28	Overtime ban	AEF	Unofficial	Demand for higher basic rate	Compromise settlement
May (12)	1 foundry: track workers and dressers	Small group	Intermittent go-slow	TGWU	Unofficial	Piece-rate demands	Varied outcome
May (13)	3 foundry: maintenance	—	Dispute was settled in discussion	TGWU	—	Dismissal of two Indian maintenance men for disobedience	Re-instated Indian

(14) June	3 foundry	—	Dispute settled in discussion	AEF	—	A.E.F. threat to walkout, due to TGWU poaching in maintenance	Agreement upon membership exchanges reached
(15) June 26th	1 foundry	—	Dispute settled in new procedure	TGWU	—	TGWU shop-steward suspended for various reasons including breach of the new procedure	District organizer got him re-instated
(16) Sept.	1 & 2 foundry	200	Strike	TGWU	Un-official	Dismissal of the same shop-steward	—

redundancy, three were over demands for dismissals or protests against reinstatement, and one was about promotion.
In addition, there was one dispute over the allocation of
work and one over poaching.

Nine of the disputes involved more than 25 workers in
sanctions and, since four were settled without sanctions, this
means that small stoppages were not typical. On the other
hand, the majority of disputes were short. There was only
one prolonged strike involving 70 men for two weeks. The
other prolonged disputes involved go-slows or overtime
bans. In addition, the dispute figures are dominated by
foundry 1, which is solely responsible for nine of the entries,
and shares in two others. Foundry 2 was involved in only
three cases, and foundry 3 in two. No sanctions were used
in foundry 3.

DISPUTES INVOLVING THE TGWU MEMBERS

In order to analyse the role of the immigrants, strikes
involving them must be separated from those involving
other workers. When this is done, certain patterns emerge.
To begin with, the immigrants have been prepared, at
times, to take action on wage issues, but at no time did a
large group of immigrants come out over a wage dispute.
The sanctions were short and on a small scale. One serious
dispute over the dismissal of an immigrant derived from an
argument with a supervisor over a piece-work question, but
this must be classed as a disciplinary dispute. The TGWU
shop-floor organization is exceptionally responsive to all the
pressures of the rank and file so that there was no oligarchic
leadership to decide what the members wanted, and yet the
immigrants apparently did not regard wage issues as serious
enough to warrant a major confrontation. The fragmentation of the wage system is one reason for the small scale of
wage disputes, but it is also likely that the immigrants did

not have very strong grievances over pay. The susceptibility of management to pressure on the piece-work system and the availability of overtime meant that, as a rule, earnings were high. In addition the incidence of recorded disputes may be a poor guide to the number of earnings grievances since these are so fragmented.

Given the complexity of the piece-work payment system, it is perhaps surprising that there were so few disputes over pay. The vast majority of disputes at Birmid Qualcast were over leapfrogging claims to gain higher earnings. Perhaps the crucial difference between the Birmid group and these foundries is that the management here was content to leave the payment system decentralized, and made no attempt to impose central control over piece-work claims. By contrast, the centralized system at Birmid led to the build-up of pressure and a rise in unconstitutional action, since the only way workers could get their claims handled quickly was to strike and make the issue an urgent one.

While wage disputes made a minor contribution to total unrest, disciplinary disputes and strikes over matters customarily determined by managerial prerogative were much more important. The most important strikes involving the TGWU were about dismissals, redundancy, transfer of work and suspension; and other disputes arose over manning and shop-stewards' rights and facilities. Several points can usefully be made about this sort of dispute. First, one reason for all these disputes was the lack of an adequate procedure for joint discussion. In addition, managerial attitudes were hardened by their view that the union had no right to interfere in this sort of question. The immigrants were breaching the customary limits of the right to bargain and this had serious repercussions on their relations with the AEF. The white workers were upset because the immigrants were flouting rules which they had accepted.

Some interesting points about the consequences of the ethnic work-units for the system of job regulation arise from examining individual disputes. In dispute number (3) at foundry 2, the dressers came out in spite of the fact that the dismissed individual was unpopular and had a weak case. What is surprising is that the whole shop came out on this issue, which turned into one of principle as to whether the agreement was being followed. This indicates something of the Indians' solidarity.

Dispute number (4) is a good example of the sort of issue that could call forth united action from the ethnic work-units. The dresser who was made redundant was a community leader, with high seniority in terms of the Indians' own values. In consequence the immigrants struck because they felt the redundancy was 'inappropriate' for this particular individual. A settlement was sought by offering the man another job on the same rate, but this was refused, one reason being that the man felt he had an established right to his previous job. Management eventually conceded.

The next strike involving the immigrants (5) was clearly a breach of established foundry custom, in that the immigrants were trying to control the allocation of work. The dispute was an expression of ethnic solidarity in the face of traditional managerial practices. The implication of the transfer was that the dressers' piece-work earnings would be reduced in one shop, in order to equalize them with earnings in the other shop. But all the TGWU members, including core-makers and others not directly involved, came out in support of the dressers.

The next strike of the immigrants (7) was another good example of the sort of problem that could arise through their not being integrated into the factory culture. On 4 April 1970 one particular dresser thought his wage packet was too small. Piece-work earnings were not calculated exactly that week, but an estimate was given and the balance, if any, was due to be paid the next week. An argument took place with a supervisor who alleged that the immigrant swore at him. The following Monday the man's time-card was arbitrarily withdrawn, without proper notice. After the shop-steward had made a brief attempt to get the decision changed, all the TGWU members walked out. Four moulders left hot metal in their ladles and were discharged for this misdemeanor. The strike was to reinstate all five men, and illustrates two interesting points. First, it shows how a misunderstanding between first-line management and immigrants can arise and escalate. Second, it demonstrated the solidarity of the immigrants over what was customarily an unexceptional managerial action.

Dispute number (10) did not result in a strike, but is a good instance of the conflict that can arise between the immigrants' norms and those of the traditional work culture. The ethnic work-units possess their own hierarchy for pro-motion to better-paid jobs, and these may conflict with management's ideas about the requisite skills and experience.

Dispute numbers (13), (15) and (16) resemble the earlier dismissal cases. Management's rough and ready methods of discipline were in conflict with the powerful loyalties of the immigrants. The final dispute, which occurred when this account was being written, followed a predictable pattern of conflict over behaviour escalating into a dismissal dispute.

The dismissal disputes usually began with an argument between a supervisor and an immigrant over a substantive issue (such as payment, the way in which a job should be done, absence or swearing), in most instances due to the immigrants' ignorance of the foundry customs. But the immigrants also ignored foundry customs in the way they conducted the discussions. For example, they were not pre-pared to compromise upon wage claims because they had

not acquired the traditional responses customary among
white workers. At one time the knock-out section in foundry
1b put in a piece-work claim that would have yielded
earnings of £50–£60 over 40 hours, and refused to
compromise until the district organizer arranged a tempo-
rary settlement for them. When ignorance of foundry
custom caused conflict, the supervisors' reaction was
generally to use their own arbitrary powers of dismissal. It
was the use of these powers that evoked the strongest
reactions from the immigrants.

In disputes numbers (4), (7), (13) and (15), the immigrants reacted against what they considered to be unfair
managerial actions. Dismissals affected the immigrants
more than the white workers, precisely because group
cohesion was so much stronger, and family and community
relations were broken by the dismissal. The rigid seniority
and the strong social bonds of the ethnic work gangs made
it more likely that they would challenge management
decisions.

Consequently most of the serious conflict between the
TGWU and management centred around disciplinary
action rather than around substantive questions.

In addition, the traditional disputes procedure was
ignored. All the strikes took place without notice, and without very much discussion to find a solution. The foundry
customs excluded strike action as a means of pressurizing
management, but the segregation of the immigrants meant
that they were not acquainted with this attitude. They did
not understand that the use of sanctions was to be avoided
if possible, and were therefore out of touch with the consensus upon which the procedure was based. In several cases
the immigrant workers were admittedly faced with perish-
able issues, where action had to be immediate to be
effective, but it remains true that they did not conform to
the traditional rules of procedure because they were not

aware of the rules, and also because they received no guidance from the guardians of tradition—the AEF.

There were also cases of minor breaches of procedure by the TGWU shop-stewards which upset both the AEF and the supervisors. For example, the immigrants took grievances straight to the managing director because they had found him helpful in the past.

While these patterns of behaviour help to explain most of the strikes, there were also exceptions. The shop-stewards in foundry 3 understood all the niceties of the informal rules. They were prepared to compromise in wage claims and controversial issues of union membership and generally conformed to traditional practices. There were also several exceptions to the general rule of immigrant solidarity. During the strike over a dismissal (7), when the TGWU stayed out for two weeks, there was some blacklegging by immigrants and some violence on the picket lines when the shop-stewards tried to enforce discipline upon the few recalcitrant members. The TGWU suffered from factionalism, which caused high turnover amongst shop-stewards and from political manoeuvring inside the joint shop-stewards' committee. There was also some evidence of conflict between the union and the community hierarchy[17], especially in foundry 1, although this never disturbed the solid front presented to management. Thus, the broad patterns of behaviour require qualification but the qualifications do not substantially affect the explanation of the strikes.

The disputes also offer some indication of union objectives. By opposing dismissals and redundancy the shop-stewards created obligations to the union, which took on the role of protector, and was able to exercise discipline over its members. The union was able thus to consolidate its authority over the ethnic work-units by acting as a guardian of the traditional customs of the immigrants. The difference

between the objectives of the TGWU and the AEF was
partly due to the difference between the two sets of
customary rules which they were trying to protect.

DISPUTES INVOLVING THE AEF AND ASTMS MEMBERS

The AEF was involved in four of the disputes listed in
Table 3, and the ASTMS in one. By 1970 the AEF had
been shocked out of its traditional individualism and con-
servatism by the erosion of the customary rules by the immigrants. Their demand for a higher basic rate (11) and their
other wage claims were attempts to re-establish differentials,
and the use of sanctions to obtain results was stimulated by
the immigrants' success. Some other AEF demands were
directly inspired by the achievements of the TGWU. For
instance, after the TGWU stewards had signed a new
disputes procedure, they were allowed to hold periodic
meetings in works' time to bring up any problems and co-
ordinate union activity. The AEF demanded the same pri-
vilege, and when management demurred, they threatened
to strike. Management described the AEF's new approach
as 'copying the militancy of the immigrants, because they
saw it paid off'.

However, most of the AEF disputes were aimed at
forcing management to take action against the immigrant
shop-stewards. The simplest case of inter-union strife was
over membership in foundry 3. The more complicated
cases involved AEF reactions against strikes by the immigrants. On two occasions the AEF held token strikes to
indicate disapproval of managerial concessions to the immigrants. The white workers approved of the management's
initial action, seeing the dismissals and transfers as appli-
cations of the traditional rules which applied to them. They
thought it was unfair that the immigrants should get away

with breaking rules which the white workers felt were appropriate. In addition, the strong disapproval of strike action felt by white workers impelled them to protest against the immigrants' behaviour. Initially the shop-stewards opposed strike action, but they were apparently swayed by the crowd at mass meetings. The behaviour of the white workers during the strikes of the immigrants is another indication of the extent of the opposition to the immigrants' behaviour. During the long strike in April 1970 the white workers worked overtime to help management resist the immigrants' demands. When the TGWU demands were met, the men in foundry 1 walked out *en masse,* but their convenor persuaded them to come back. They struck the next day instead. The white workers did not display anything like the same cohesion in their own disputes as they showed in these protests against the immigrants.

The sole ASTMS dispute was on similar lines. When the immigrant workers developed ethnic work gangs the supervisors and foremen found their traditional role undermined. These gangs were difficult to discipline and control so that the supervisors became a depressed class. Not only was their authority threatened, but their earnings differentials were eroded. Their quality was low and their problems were aggravated by lack of industrial relations training. They joined ASTMS because they felt that top management would not support them against the shop-floor militants, and their fears were justified. The strike was an expression of solidarity with a supervisor who had been sworn at, and then coerced into accepting an apology. Higher management's concern to maintain production conflicted with the supervisors' desire to maintain their authority. The supervisors and the senior members of the AEF had a great deal in common. Supervisors tended to be promoted shop-stewards or senior workers and thus shared the customary norms, and each understood the behaviour

E

of the other. This may explain the similarity of the reactions of the two unions to the actions of the TGWU members and shop-stewards.

The ASTMS was also involved in claims for overtime pay and recognition. Both of them involved complicated negotiations, but these are irrelevant to an examination the role of the immigrants in causing the disruption of custom and practice.

6

The New Procedural Agreement:
A Postscript

After the spate of disputes in 1970 the negotiating machinery experienced several important changes, largely because management thought that some of the responsibility for the disputes lay with the old inadequate procedure. They also felt that in some magical way a recurrence of open conflict would be prevented by the signing of an agreement containing an obligation not to strike until all possible means of avoiding the strike had been taken. The agreement covering the handling of disputes was signed in June. It provided for arbitration by the Department of Employment as a final stage, and also covered discipline, recognition and the check-off of union dues for the TGWU. These rules applied to the TGWU alone though management also began negotiations with the AEF because the old informal understandings did not appear to be very reliable any more. The development of a formal procedure may be seen as a step in the right direction for the avoidance of future conflict, but it was not an inevitable consequence of the disputes which had occurred. Management could equally have reacted by pretending that nothing was wrong with the rules, and trying to get rid of the TGWU. No detailed account of the development of these formal procedural rules is given here, but several points should be made about the agreement and the nature of negotiations during the strikes.

The agreement was the product of managerial pressure. It is TGWU policy to try to get domestic procedural agreements as soon as recognition is granted, and they had managed to get an agreement covering foundry 2 in 1968. However, the other foundries had no agreements, and the proposal to introduce them took shape only during negotiations between the top management and the district organizer during the two-week strike in April. The form of the agreement was largely determined by the TGWU District Organizer, but in most respects his words accorded with management's wish, to provide a means of avoiding strikes. It appeared to resolve the problems that had led to the prolonging of the April strike and to remove the causes of several other 'wildcat' strikes. During these disputes, management condemned the TGWU because they had 'broken the procedure', but in fact the TGWU was not bound by a formal procedure, and had no firm commitment to the informal procedure. Procedures to avoid disputes work only if there is substantial consensus upon what is acceptable behaviour, and in the absence of a strong informal consensus it is unwise to expect informal procedure to provide universal solutions.

The establishment of a voluntary procedure should achieve two things. First, it should clarify the joint rules on handling disputes. Secondly, it should have an educative effect in showing both parties how they can avoid strikes. In fact, the new agreement did not specify in close detail what the new patterns of behaviour should be. Although the section upon behaviour in the event of a failure to agree is clear, the sections upon discipline fail to define what punishments are appropriate for specific offences. After the signing of the agreement, conflict centred on the extent of shop stewards' facilities, and it is unlikely that this would have occurred if these facilities had been defined.

On the other hand the agreement helped to educate the

Indian shop-steward, and those managers who had been ignorant about what sort of behaviour conformed to the customary rules. To some extent the agreement codified the rules that had been followed informally, and the process of negotiating and signing the agreement helped the immigrant shop-stewards to learn what their obligations were.

7

Conclusions

What the preceding chapters have done is to establish the course of events at the foundries. The logic of the course of events is sufficiently close to the chronology for the main threads of the argument to be apparent without much further analysis. The first sections show how job regulation was largely governed by custom-and-practice rules. The workability of these rules depended upon consensus between management and the workers and shop-stewards, which existed prior to the growth of the TGWU. Since the AEF tended to be both weak and conservative there was no other union to act as a focus for resentment. The following sections show how the ethnic units operated in the foundries and how the TGWU fitted in with their behaviour. At this stage the latent causes of conflict were apparent. The next section (on disputes) reveals the particular areas of custom which led to conflict between management and the immigrants. The subsequent move towards formal rules arose out of the realization by both management and the union full-time officer that the consensus upon which the informal system had been based was no longer present.

Several factors led to the collapse of the shared understanding which had operated for so long. These included turnover of management and labour and economic pressures, but this study has concentrated upon the racial factors.

In the introduction, two different conceptual approaches

in the sociology of race relations were distinguished. One is the immigrant–host framework, which treats colour as an unimportant factor in explaining immigrants' absorption. The other is the racial approach, which treats perceived racial differences as of primary importance in explaining race relations, and is closely linked with the notion of 'prejudice'. The study has made no reference to 'prejudice'. This is not because the foundries were free of individuals, some of them influential, who held attitudes that could be classed as racially prejudiced, but because their actions can be explained in terms of stated rational ends. Thus, for instance, the shop-steward in foundry 1a who disliked immigrants stated his objections to them in terms of their breach of foundry custom. In other words prejudice can be explained best in terms of social relationship. As Rex and Moore have argued:

> What we have to do is not merely classify behaviour as prejudiced but to understand the part which customs, beliefs, norms and expectation play in a larger structure, be it the structure of an ethnic minority group or that of the overall urban society, marked as it is by diverse inter-group conflicts.[18]

The immigrant–host approach treats racial relationships as part of an overall pattern of assimilation, in which the immigrants adapt to the host society until they learn the accepted patterns of behaviour. It can easily suggest that complete assimilation is a state entirely free of conflict, and tends to pose such managerial questions as, 'what are acceptable quotas of immigrants?' and 'what sort of training do they need to fit them for employment?' Rex and Moore have argued that existing studies using this approach have underestimated the internal conflicts and complexities of the host culture, and have assumed that the only sort of host–immigrant relationships that can exist must fit into a narrowly conceived pattern. In this pattern, the immigrant moves from one culture to another and goes through several stages in acquiring the host culture. They show, furthermore, how market relationships in which immigrants are involved (such as employment relationships) can be transformed into power relationships by the concentration of power within groups. Power relationships can become stabilized by a process of informal collective bargaining, and a number of different inter-racial relationships can become settled patterns. Such relationships could vary from complete integration to a caste system. To put it crudely, the absorption theorists have had too simple a view of the structural processes affecting integration. They have not been aware of the social forces that could yield different equilibrium situations.

This study does not claim to show what the final state of assimilation in a particular area of race relations is, or should be. It shows that, in employment at least, a number of different situations are possible. One occurs when a self-reinforcing set of forces maintains the isolation and independence of the immigrant. Ethnic work-units can become stable primary groups in which the immigrant culture is preserved. The stability of this form of organization is incompatible with the crude version of the absorption thesis. Different relationships can, however, be discerned. In foundry 3, for instance, the immigrants had not become settled into self-contained groups, and were partly absorbed. Some immigrants were in the white workers' union, the AEF, and others were in jobs such as truck-driving and maintenance which involved mixing with white workers. The white and coloured workers were more intermingled in foundry 3 than in the others, and here there was no conflict over custom likely to stabilize barriers between the groups.

However, the cultural factors emphasized by the immigrant–host approach can provide a clue to the sources of conflict between the immigrants and the white workers and managers. The conflict that occurred in the foundries arose because the immigrants' norms affecting industrial relations could not be maintained in isolation. Industrial relations rules depend for their existence upon their general acceptance by all concerned. The breach of foundry custom by the immigrants and the attempts to establish their own customs directly disturbed established patterns of rules. It is difficult for immigrants to set up self-contained communities in employment because of the importance of common rules. Employment stands in contrast to housing in this respect, since conflict between immigrants and white residents is likely to occur only upon the fringes of residential communities.

In such a situation, custom-and-practice rules are more unstable than other kinds of rules, such as managerial unilateral rules or collective agreements. Both these other categories of rules are communicable and comprehensive, whereas custom-and-practice rules are not. They arise out of rational decision-making, and in consequence someone is responsible for communicating and enforcing them. The origins of custom are however so indeterminate that it may not be evident that a rule exists until it is broken. Thus a custom-and-practice rule must generally be learnt through contact with those who observe it. In ethnic work-units the immigrant is isolated and such contact is not provided.

The system of job regulation at the foundries was about as unsuitable for immigrants as it could be. The dominance of custom and practice and the absence of channels of communication and education meant that it was difficult for the immigrants to come to terms with the customs peculiar to foundry work. Management made no attempt to soften the possible causes of conflict by trying to integrate the immigrants or by making the system of job regulation more comprehensible. As a result, the foundries were necessarily prone to conflict from racial factors.

References

(1) ALLAN FLANDERS, *Industrial Relations: What is Wrong with the System?* (London, Faber, 1965).

(2) ALLAN FLANDERS, *The Fawley Productivity Agreements* (London, Faber, 1964). Examples of this sort of custom and practice are given.

(3) ORVIS COLLINS, MELVILLE DALTON AND DONALD ROY, 'Restrictions of Output and Social Cleavage in Industry', *Applied Anthropology*, Vol. 5, Summer 1946.

(4) WILLIAM BROWN, *A Consideration of Custom and Practice*, Industrial Relations Research Unit discussion paper (University of Warwick, 1971). This contains a full discussion of the legitimacy of custom and practice.

(5) A. I. MARSH, *Disputes Procedures and British Industry*, Royal Commission Research Paper, No. 2, Part 1 (H.M.S.O., 1966).

(6) ALLAN FLANDERS AND ALLAN FOX, 'The Reform of Collective Bargaining: From Donovan to Durkheim', *British Journal of Industrial Relations*, Vol. VII, No. 2, July 1969.

(7) PETER MARSH, *Anatomy of a Strike* (Institute of Race Relations Special, 1967).
PAUL FOOT, 'The Strike at Courtaulds, Preston,' Supplement to *Institute of Race Relations Newsletter* (July, 1965).

(8) S. N. EISENSTADT, *The Absorption of Immigrants* (London, Routledge & Kegan Paul, 1954).
SHEILA PATTERSON, *Immigrants in Industry* (Oxford, O.U.P. for the Institute of Race Relations, 1969).
PETER L. WRIGHT, *The Coloured Worker in British Industry* (Oxford, O.U.P. for the Institute of Race Relations, 1968).
These works are the best known using this approach. See also DENNIS BROOKS, *The Absorption of Immigrants in London Transport* (forthcoming.)

(9) BERYL RADIN, 'Coloured Workers and the British Trade Unions', *Race*, VIII (2) (1966). She examines some of the problems of discrimination in trade unions. The study of shop-floor practices is, however, weak. A more useful recent study is, SHEILA ALLEN, 'Immigrants or Workers,' *Race and Racialism*, ed. Sami Zubaida (London, Tavistock, 1970).

(10) WRIGHT, op. cit. (note 8).

(11) COMMISSION ON INDUSTRIAL RELATIONS (C.I.R.), *Report No. 4, Birmid Qualcast*, Cmnd. 4264 (H.M.S.O., 1970).

(12) A. I. MARSH, *Industrial Relations in Engineering* (London, Pergamon Press, 1965). This gives an account of the operation of National Engineering Agreements.

(13) H. A. TURNER, *Trade Union Growth, Structure and Policy* (London, George Allen and Unwin, 1962) p. 51.

(14) PETER MARSH, op. cit. (note 7).

(15) BERYL RADIN, op. cit. (note 9).

(16) DE WITT JOHN, *The Indian Workers' Association* (Oxford, O.U.P. for the Institute of Race Relations, 1969). This gives an account of the role of the Indian Workers Association amongst Punjabi trade unionists.

(17) DE WITT JOHN, op. cit. (note 16) and PETER MARSH, op. cit. (note 7).

(18) JOHN REX and ROBERT MOORE, *Race, Community and Conflict* (Oxford O.U.P. for the Institute of Race Relations, 1967), p. 13.

I3